C000241239

Colour Mixing Swatch Book

by Michael Wilcox

The Michael Wilcox School of Colour
Artist Quality products created by Artists

SCHOOL OF COLOUR PUBLICATIONS
www.schoolofcolour.com

ISBN UK 0-9679628-4-6
ISBN USA 0-9679628-5-4
Text, Illustrations and arrangement Copyright:
The Michael Wilcox School of Colour Ltd.
First published 2001
Colour scanning and balancing: Gary Hatcher
Planning: Chris Dorey
Finishing: Maureen Bonas
Artwork: Jeremy Ford
Coordination: Anne Gardner

Contents

The colour swatches

The swatches were all prepared by mixing colour A with colour B. The resulting mixes * are shown between these two colours on the top line.

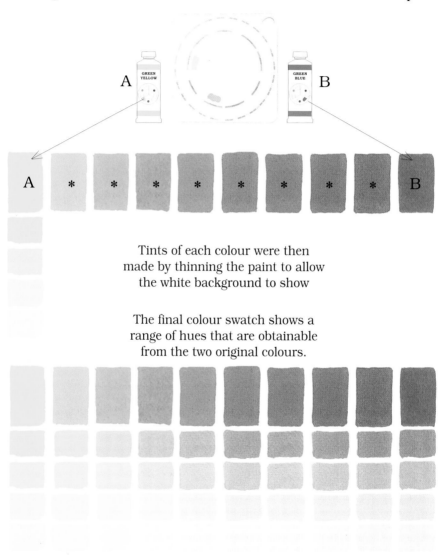

Tints of each colour were then made by thinning the paint to allow the white background to show

The final colour swatch shows a range of hues that are obtainable from the two original colours.

To mix selected colours

Hansa Yellow and Cerulean Blue

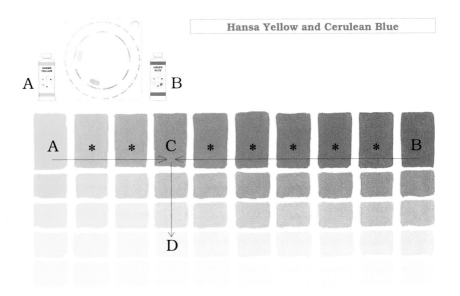

If you wished, for example, to mix colour D, simply mix colours A and B to arrive at C. Then thin the colour until you have D.

The names of the actual colours that you need are given in the title bar at the top of the page, in this case Hansa Yellow and Cerulean Blue have been used.

Important note

Conventional colour printing is severely limited when it comes to the depiction of the range of hues available in paint form. Therefore please treat the colour mixes given in this book as a guide rather than as an exact match.
In addition, the colours supplied by the various paint manufacturers vary widely.
It would be impossible to produce such a book which covered all possibilities exactly.

The brightest tints are created when the background lightens the colour.

The use of white will always dull and 'cool' a colour.

The tints shown throughout this book are produced by thinning the colour with a dilutent (water, turpentine etc.) and applying the paint lightly.

This approach will give the brightest tint and is applicable to oil paints, acrylics and alkyds, as well as to watercolour paints.

The oil and acrylic painter should perhaps consider this approach rather than, as is usual, only adding white.

When white is added to any colour it will dull and 'cool' it. It will also make otherwise transparent paints more opaque and 'chalky'.

However, such colours have a very important part to play in all forms of colour use. The swatches show only the brighter tints which are available as it is easy to imagine them made slightly duller and 'chalkier though the use of white.

5

The position of each colour used in this book is given on the Colour Mixing Palette developed by the School of Colour. However, it is not essential that you use the palette as any mixing surface will do. If you do use the palette the diagrams will help in placing the colours.

CADMIUM RED LIGHT

ORANGE-RED, OPAQUE
LIGHTFASTNESS I: EXCELLENT
P.R. 108
It is suggested that you avoid genuine
Vermilion as an alternative as it can darken
quite dramatically.

QUINACRIDONE VIOLET

VIOLET-RED, TRANSPARENT
LIGHTFASTNESS II: VERY GOOD
P.V. 19
Alizarin Crimson should not be used as an
alternative as it fades when applied thinly or mixed
with white. It also gives poor violets.

CADMIUM YELLOW LIGHT

ORANGE-YELLOW, OPAQUE
LIGHTFASTNESS I: EXCELLENT
P.Y 35
Avoid Chrome Yellow as a possible alternative
as it tends to darken on exposure to light.

HANSA YELLOW LIGHT

GREEN-YELLOW, SEMI TRANSPARENT
LIGHTFASTNESS II: VERY GOOD
P.Y. 3
Other green-yellows will be suitable if they
are lightfast. The most common name will
be 'Lemon Yellow'

CERULEAN BLUE

GREEN-BLUE, OPAQUE
LIGHTFASTNESS I: EXCELLENT
P.B. 36:1
It pays to use genuine Cerulean Blue as alternatives
are usually inferior imitations.
Check that the pigment is either PB 36:1 or PB35

ULTRAMARINE BLUE

VIOLET-BLUE, TRANSPARENT
LIGHTFASTNESS I: EXCELLENT
P.B. 29
It always pays to use a quality Ultramarine. Inferior
versions will not give clear, even layers when
applied thinly due to an excess of filler.

The colours suggested on this and the next page have been carefully selected to give as wide a range of lightfast colours as possible. School of Colour paints were used to prepare the colour mixes but any brand can be used. Do bear in mind however, that different makes tend to vary somewhat in colour. One manufacturers' Cadmium Yellow Light, for example, might be brighter and more orange than another. As this book is intended to be a guide this should not present a problem.
It would be impossible to cover all variations

YELLOW OCHRE

NEUTRALISED ORANGE-YELLOW,
SEMI-OPAQUE
LIGHTFASTNESS I: EXCELLENT
P.Y. 43
A good quality Yellow Ochre will cover well, (semi-opaque) but also give quite clear thinner layers.

RAW SIENNA

NEUTRALISED ORANGE-YELLOW,
SEMI-TRANSPARENT
LIGHTFASTNESS I: EXCELLENT
P.Br. 7
Look for the ingredients 'P.Br 7 Raw Sienna' as this colour is often imitated.

PHTHALOCYANINE BLUE

GREEN-BLUE, TRANSPARENT
LIGHTFASTNESS II: VERY GOOD
P.B.15
Prussian Blue could be used as an alternative to Phthalocyanine Blue as it is similar in hue, transparency and strength.

PHTHALOCYANINE GREEN

MID-GREEN, TRANSPARENT
LIGHTFASTNESS I: EXCELLENT
P.G. 36
Viridian would be a suitable alternative as it is similar in colour, transparency and strength to Phthalocyanine Green.

BURNT SIENNA

NEUTRALISED ORANGE, TRANSPARENT
LIGHTFASTNESS I: EXCELLENT
P.Br. 7
As with all transparent colours it pays to use a good quality as inferior versions often contain an excess of filler.

WHITE, OPAQUE

TITANIUM WHITE
LIGHTFASTNESS I: EXCELLENT
P.W.6
Choose your white according to appropiate media.

The pigment/s used in a paint can be identified by what is known as the 'Colour Index Name'
For example, the pigment used in genuine Phthalocyanine Green (above) is P.G. 36.
This stands for 'Pigment Green 36'.

Although the mixes shown in the book are produced from just 11 colours, 12 are mentioned on the cover as you may choose to use white to create your tints when actually mixing the colours.
Please see page 5

Hansa Yellow and Cerulean Blue

A range of bright greens which vary in transparency from the semi transparent green-yellow to the opaque green-blue. Why buy pre-mixed greens when they are so easy to prepare?

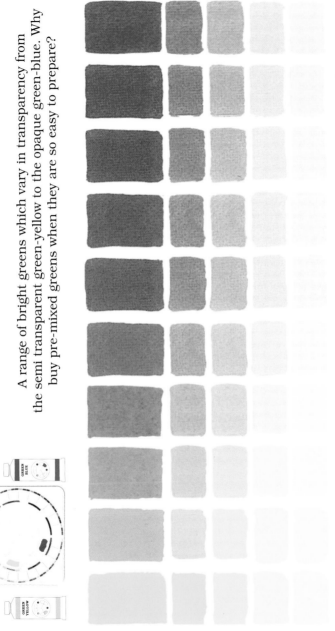

Hansa Yellow and Ultramarine Blue

Useful mid intensity greens. As the yellow is semi-transparent and the blue is very transparent, the tints will be particularly clear. Green-yellow to violet-blue.

Cadmium Yellow Light and Cerulean Blue

Further mid intensity greens. Both the yellow and the blue are opaque. At full strength the mixes cover well but tend to lose clarity when thinly applied due to the opacity of the contributing colours.

Cadmium Yellow Light and Ultramarine Blue

From dull opaque yellow greens to dulled semi transparent blue greens. A range of very useful landscape colours. An ideal way to mix deep, subdued greens.

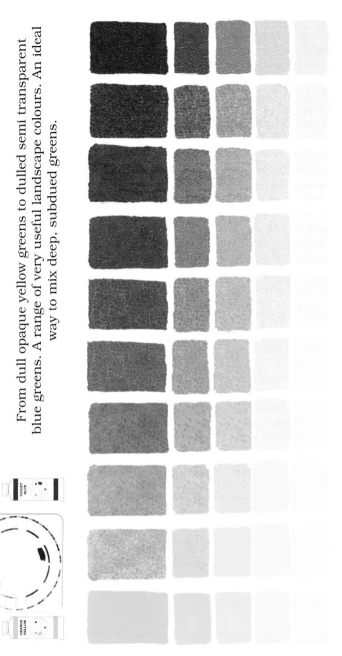

Hansa Yellow and Phthalocyanine Blue

A range of clear bright greens which will be more intense in paint form than shown printed here. Semi-transparent green-yellow to very transparent green-blue. The tints will wash out very thinly.

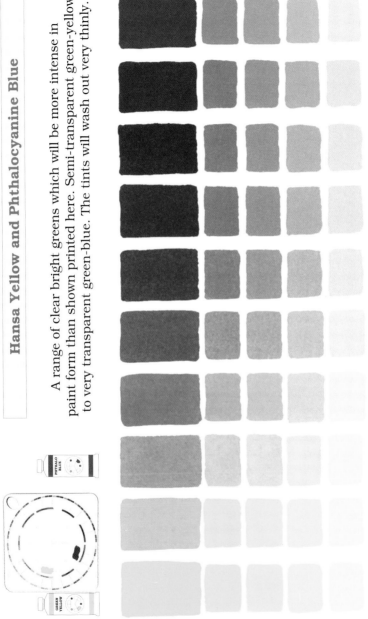

Hansa Yellow and Phthalocyanine Green

From a semi-transparent green-yellow to the very transparent Phthalocyanine Green. A valuable range of clear, very bright greens. Phthalocyanine Green is very intense and should be used with care.

14

Cadmium Yellow and Phthalocyanine Green

Being an orange-yellow the Cadmium Yellow Light will bring very little green to the mixes. From opaque yellow, to semi-opaque mid greens and on to transparent bright green.

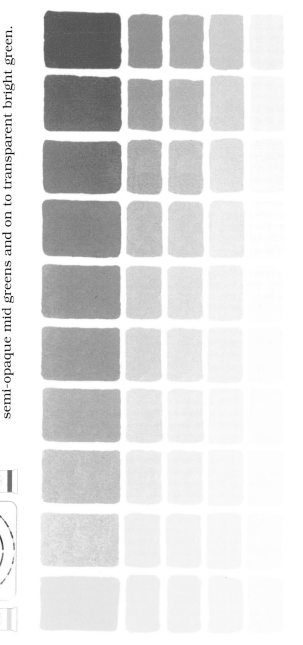

Cerulean Blue and Phthalocyanine Green

As the blue is opaque and the green very transparent these mixes will change in opacity, becoming more transparent towards the green end of the range. An important factor in colour use.

Ultramarine Blue and Phthalocyanine Green

As both colours are very transparent the mixes will give particularly clear tints. A range of slightly subdued blue greens with many applications, particularly in seascape painting.

Yellow Ochre and Ultramarine Blue

Very deep, blackish greens emerge from these two poor 'carriers' of green. In thinner applications these hues give a series of very subtle tints. Such colours are difficult to reproduce conventionally.

Raw Sienna and Ultramarine Blue

Raw Sienna is a soft neutral orange-yellow varying between transparent and semi-transparent. Very soft greens emerge from these two hues which are particularly useful in glazing.

Phthalocyanine Green and Phthalocyanine Blue

For the brightest possible mixed transparent greens. Intense colours which give very clear tints when lightly applied. Both colours are strong and should be used with care when mixing with other hues.

Quinacridone violet and Phthalocyanine Green

As both contributing colours are transparent and also mixing complementaries, expect very dark coloured greys around the middle of the range when the mixes are at all heavily applied.

Quinacridone Violet and Ultramarine Blue

Red to blue violets; bright, strong and very transparent, the brightest lightfast violets that can be mixed. The results will be much duller and will turn bluer as the red fades if you use unreliable Alizarin Crimson.

Cadmium Red Light and Ultramarine Blue

A range of mid intensity violets will emerge as these two are mixed as only the blue is a good 'carrier' of violet. The blends will vary in opacity from the opaque red to the transparent blue.

Quinacridone Violet and Cerulean Blue

Further mid intensity violets. This time only the red 'carries' a useful 'amount' of violet, the blue reflects very little. From transparent violet red to opaque green-blue.

Cadmium Red Light and Cerulean Blue

Dulled violets around the middle of the range with subdued orange reds and green-blues at either end. As both colours are opaque the full strength mixes will cover other colours very well.

Cadmium Yellow Light and Cadmium Red Light

Bright yellow to red oranges. Both colours are strong and opaque, these qualities will be imparted to the mixes. The colours that you mix, if you select quality paints, will be slightly brighter than shown here.

Hansa Yellow and Cadmium Red Light

Useful mid intensity oranges. The red 'carries' most of the orange to the mix with the yellow providing very little. The blends will be neither dull or particularly bright.

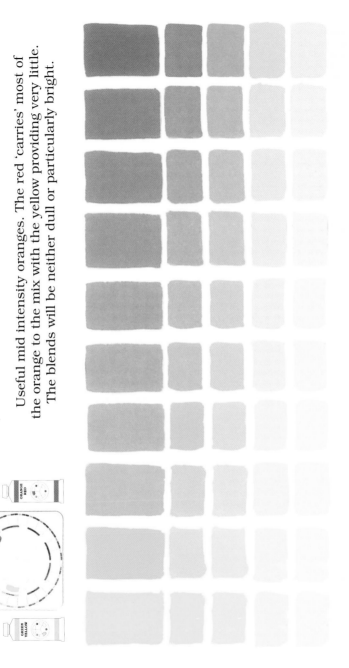

Cadmium Yellow Light and Quinacridone Violet

A valuable range of mid intensity oranges. As only the orange-yellow is an efficient 'carrier' of orange, the mixes will be neither dull or particularly bright. Opaque at the yellow end moving to transparent violet-red.

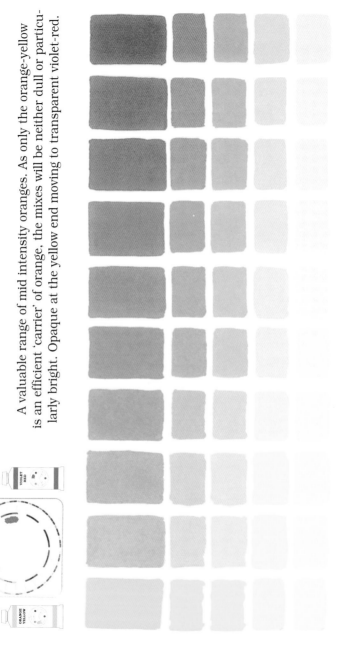

Hansa Yellow and Quinacridone Violet

From the semi-transparent green-yellow to the very clear violet-red, the mixes can be considered to be transparent. As neither colour brings much orange to the mix the blends will be rather dull.

Yellow Ochre and Cadmium Red Light

Yellow Ochre covers well when heavily applied but gives reasonably transparent thinner layers. Soft, subdued oranges which all work very well together.

Mixing the greens for the following colour swatches

Hansa Yellow and Cerulean Blue

Mixed yellow-green; pages 35 & 36

Mixed bright green; pages 32 & 33
Use either green as a guide.

Mixed blue -green; pages 38 & 39

Please refer to page 9 (partly reproduced above) if you wish to mix the greens for the following colour swatches. Do not try to match the colours exactly. In the first place you will be using paints and these are printed colours. In the second, this swatch book is intended as a colour mixing *guide*, not as an exact colour matching resource. Very close matching could only ever apply to one range of paints, would be prohibitively expensive to print and would still be far from exact. Please bear these factors in mind when working with this guide.

Cadmium Red Light and mixed bright green

As with all of the colour ranges in this book, these hues can be made to harmonise with ease. Opaque orange-red to bright greens with very subtle coloured greys, particularly when thinly applied.

Quinacridone Violet and mixed bright green

Soft coloured greys, neutral reds and greens. The range moves from transparent violet-red to a semi-opaque green. Red and green are visual as well as mixing complementaries. Very subtle tints.

GREEN YELLOW

GREEN BLUE

VIOLET RED

For those using our colour coded mixing palette:

The outer ring of mixing wells are intended for those colours that you wish to neutralise (darken or make duller). To produce the yellow-green for the following two swatches, simply mix the green following the guidelines on page 31 and place it into the nearest outer well. As you will see, the outer wells are all colour coded. As you will be mixing a bright, rather than a light or dark yellow-green, use the centre colour on the well as your guidance. Do not try to match the colour that you have mixed and the colour printed on the palette. So many yellow-greens could be mixed that it would be impossible to have a well for each.

Mixed yellow green and Cadmium Red Light

As the mixed green can be considered to be semi-opaque, and the red is fully opaque, the mixes will cover well. If the fully saturated red and green are used sparingly, the entire range can be harmonised with ease.

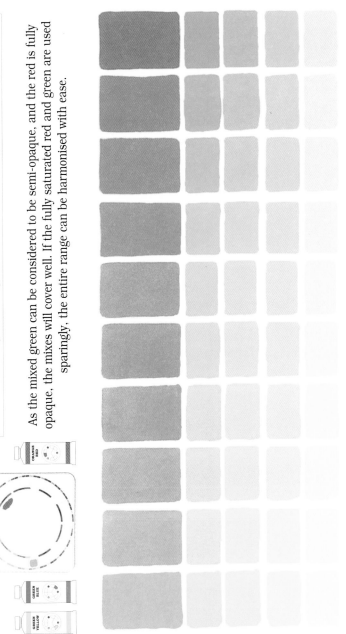

Mixed yellow green and Quinacridone Violet

The mixed green will be relatively bright as the blue and yellow are both efficient carriers of green. Yellow-green and violet-red make a versatile mixing pair giving a wide range of colours to work with.

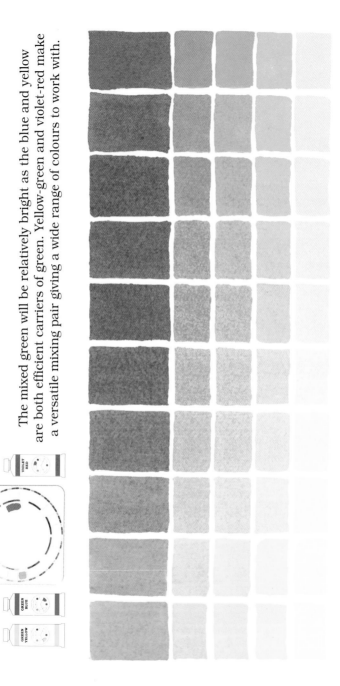

Using the outer wells of the Mixing Palette

For those using our colour coded mixing palette:

The outer ring of mixing wells are intended for those colours that you wish to neutralise (darken or make duller). To produce the blue-green for the following two swatches, simply mix the green following the guidelines on page 31 and place it into the nearest outer well. As already mentioned, do not try to match the colour that you have mixed and the colour printed on the palette.

The palette has been designed to identify the mixing complementaries. These will always be found opposite each other. By placing the colour into the nearest colour coded well and looking to the opposite side of the palette you will see that the complementary of a blue-green is an orange-red.

Mixed blue green and Cadmium Red Light

A most useful complementary pair. They neutralise (dull) each other beautifully, give versatile coloured greys around the middle of the range and an extensive series of subtle tints.

Mixed blue green and Quinacridone Violet

The semi-transparent Hansa Yellow together with the opaque Cerulean Blue will give semi-opaque blue greens. The mixes will become progressively more transparent towards the violet red.

39

Mixing the violets for the following colour swatches

Quinacridone Violet and Ultramarine Blue

Mixed blue-violet for further experimentation

Mixed bright violet; pages 41 & 42
Use either violet as a guide.

Mixed red-violet for further experimentation

Please refer to page 22 (partly reproduced above) if you wish to mix the violets for the following colour swatches. As has been mentioned, do not try to match the colours exactly. If you wish to experiment further, try adding red or blue-violet to either type of yellow (Hansa Yellow or the Cadmium Yellow Light).

Cadmium Yellow Light and mixed bright Violet

Semi-transparent, coloured greys will emerge around the centre of the range as the yellow and violet absorb each others light. Being a complementary mixing pair the two colours will absorb each other.

Hansa Yellow and mixed bright Violet

As the yellow is changed from an opaque orange yellow to a semi-transparent green-yellow, so the results will alter dramatically when compared to the mixes on the previous page.

Mixing the oranges for the following colour swatches

Cadmium Yellow Light and Cadmium Red Light

Mixed yellow-orange for further experimentation

Mixed bright-orange; pages 44 & 45
Use either orange as a guide.

Mixed red-orange for further experimentation

Please refer to page 26 (partly reproduced above) if you wish to mix the oranges for the following colour swatches. As has been mentioned, do not try to match the colours exactly. If you wish to experiment further, try adding yellow-orange or red-orange to any of the blues. (Cerulean Blue, Ultramarine Blue or Phthalocyanine Blue).

43

Mixed bright orange and Cerulean Blue

As both the orange and blue are opaque, the mixes will cover other colours well. Subtle coloured greys and tints emerge around centre of the range. Invaluable coloured greys when mixed to order.

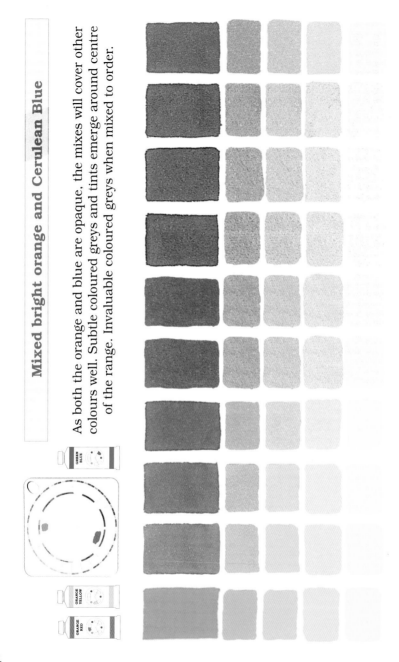

Mixed bright orange and Ultramarine Blue

Being a complementary mixing pair they will absorb each others' light. This leads to the dark coloured greys around the centre of the range. Such dark colours are invaluable when they can be produced to order.

Cerulean Blue and Burnt Sienna

The coloured greys around the middle of the range will not be quite so dark as the mixes on the next two pages, because the Cerulean Blue is opaque and the mixes will absorb less light.

Phthalocyanine Blue and Burnt Sienna

A very useful range of transparent colours which can be harmonised with ease. Expect deep coloured greys, almost blacks, as the two colours absorb each other and the light sinks in deeply.

Ultramarine Blue and Burnt Sienna

Being mixing complementaries the two colours will absorb each other, creating darks. As they are both transparent even more light will be lost. The ideal replacement for black, Payne's Grey and possibly Burnt Umber.

Cerulean Blue and Ultramarine Blue

Invaluable blues will result from mixes of the opaque green-blue and the transparent violet-blue. Not only will the colour change but so also will the transparency, the violet-blues giving much clearer tints if applied thinly and without white.

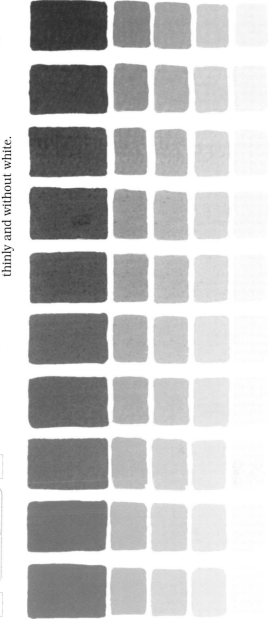

Cerulean Blue and Phthalocyanine Blue

From the opaque green-blue (Cerulean Blue) to the transparent green blue, Phthalocyanine Blue, a superb range of 'sky' colours will emerge. Semi-transparent blues around the middle of the range.

Phthalocyanine Blue and Ultramarine Blue

Transparent green-blue to transparent violet-blue. Many imitation Cobalt Blues (few are genuine nowadays) are produced from one or the other of these two, with the addition of white. A range of clear, bright blues.

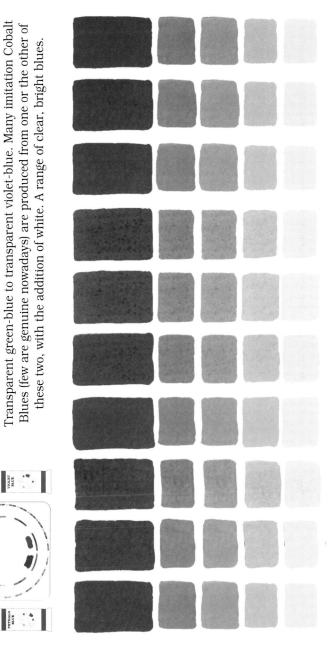

Hansa Yellow and Cadmium Yellow Light

The differences between the mixes will be very slight but they will extend your repertoire. Between the semi-transparent green-yellow (Hansa) and the opaque orange-yellow a versatile range will be available.

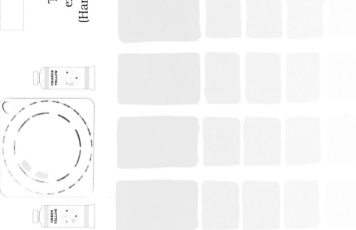

Hansa Yellow and Raw Sienna

A series of muted semi-transparent yellow oranges from this pair.
The full range can be harmonised with ease when working in monotone.
Very thin washes are possible.

Cadmium Red Light and Quinacridone Violet

From opaque orange-reds moving through semi-transparent reds to transparent violet-reds. An invaluable range. You do not need to go out and buy every red in sight.

Colour Harmony

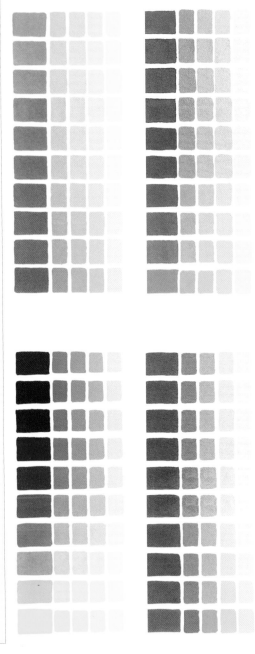

The easiest way to achieve colour harmony is to work with a very limited number of colours. The fewer the better in almost every case. As each of the colour swatches shown in the book are produced from no more than two colours, the hues on the entire page can be harmonised with ease. (The pre-mixed oranges, violets and greens can be considered a single colour as they are easily reproduced). Each swatch will give a wide range with which to work, especially where the mixing complementaries have been used, yellow and violet, blue and orange and red and green. This is because coloured greys (the darks around the middle of the blend) will give a wider range of values to work with.

The School of Colour

A range of products has been designed and books and courses published to help bring about a fuller understanding of colour and technique. We offer paints, mixing palettes, books, courses, videos, workbooks and our own range of brushes. Membership of the School of Colour is free and is available to all with an interest in colour.

Please contact any of the offices listed below.

**THE MICHAEL WILCOX
SCHOOL OF COLOR USA**

25 Mauchly #328

Irvine

CA 92618 USA

Tel: 949 450 0266

Fax: 949 450 0268

Free Phone: 1888 7 WILCOX

e-mail wilcoxsoc@earthlink.net

**THE MICHAEL WILCOX
SCHOOL OF COLOUR UK**

Gibbet Lane

Whitchurch, Bristol

BS14 OBX

United Kingdom

Tel: 01275 835500

Fax: 01275 892659

e-mail: wilcoxsoc@aol.com

**THE MICHAEL WILCOX
SCHOOL OF COLOUR
AUSTRALIA**

PO Box 516

Wanneroo 6065

Western Australia

Tel/Fax 61 8 9306 9887

e-mail:

wilcoxsoc@iinet.net.au

www.schoolofcolor.com